New

Trapped!

**by
Griselda Gifford**

Illustrated by
Beryl Sanders

Chapter 1: Nowhere to play.   page 3
Chapter 2: The secret camp   page 7
Chapter 3: Waiting for Max.   page 11
Chapter 4: Trapped!   page 15
Chapter 5: Escape   page 19
Chapter 6: A great idea!   page 24
When I'm grown up   page 32

Nelson

Thomas Nelson and Sons Ltd
Nelson House   Mayfield Road
Walton-on-Thames   Surrey
KT12 5PL   UK

51 York Place
Edinburgh
EH1 3JD   UK

Thomas Nelson (Hong Kong) Ltd
Toppan Building 10/F
22A Westlands Road
Quarry Bay   Hong Kong

Thomas Nelson Australia
102 Dodds Street
South Melbourne
Victoria 3205   Australia

Nelson Canada
1120 Birchmount Road
Scarborough Ontario
M1K 5G4   Canada

© Macmillan Education Ltd 1987
This edition © Thomas Nelson & Sons Ltd 1992
Editorial Consultant: Donna Bailey
'Trapped!' was written by Griselda Gifford and illustrated by Beryl Sanders
'When I'm grown up' was written by Peggy Clulow and illustrated by
Joyce Smith and David Dowland

First published by Macmillan Education Ltd 1987
ISBN 0-333-41895-6

This edition published by Thomas Nelson and Sons Ltd 1992

ISBN 0-17-400621-7
NPN 9 8 7 6 5

All rights reserved. No paragraph of this publication may be reproduced, copied
or transmitted save with written permission or in accordance with the provisions
of the Copyright, Design and Patents Act 1988, or under the terms of any
licence permitting limited copying issued by the Copyright Licensing Agency,
90 Tottenham Court Road, London W1P 9HE.

Any person who does any unauthorised act in relation to this publication may be
liable to criminal prosecution and civil claims for damages.

Printed in Hong Kong

Chapter 1: Nowhere to play

It was a wet day. Ben and his friend Max were playing in the living-room. There were cars all over the floor. Ben's train-set was laid out. The lines went under the chairs and a pile of books made a tunnel. Comics were mixed up with Lego. The boys had built a camp out of a chair, a table and a blanket. They sat inside eating crisps.

Ben saw Mum's feet as she came into the room. Now there would be trouble!

"What a mess!" she said. "You must tidy it up at once! Why don't you play in your bedroom, Ben?"

"It's too small to lay out the train-set," said Ben. "And it's too wet to go out. We must have somewhere to play."

"Sorry, but you will have to clear it up all the same," Mum said.

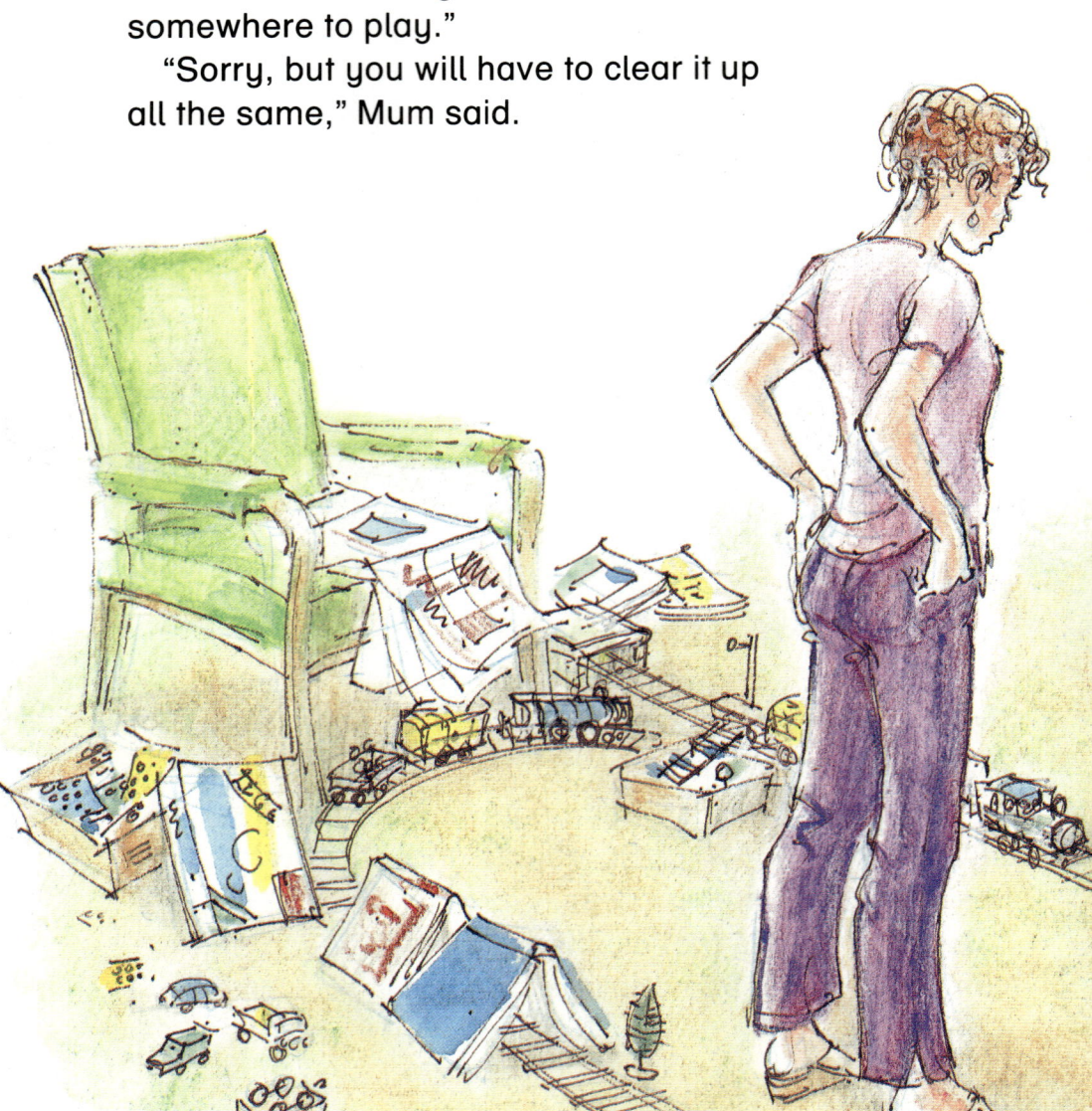

Mum went back to work in the paper shop she ran with Ben's father. They sold newspapers, cards and stationery.
They lived in a flat above the shop.

Max lived in the house next door.
His parents had a fruit shop.
They lived in the rooms above the shop.
Max had very little room for playing too.
His mother always made him put his toys away.

The boys took down the camp and put away the train-set. They knocked down the garages and the tunnel they had built.

"Where can we play?" asked Max.

Ben brushed the crisp crumbs under the sofa.

"I know!" he said. "Let's go up to the roof!"

Ben always had the ideas.

Chapter 2: The secret camp

"We can't climb on the roof," Max said.

"No, stupid! We will go up into the attic," Ben said. "There is a ladder. Come on!"

Ben ran into the hall. The ladder to the attic was hooked up to the ceiling of the hall. Ben stood on a chair and unhooked it. He pulled the ladder down.

"What about your Mum and Dad?" asked Max. "Do they let you go up to the attic?"

"They will be busy now until the shop closes," said Ben. "They won't know. It will be our secret place."

"Our attic is full of junk," said Max. "Nobody goes up there."

Ben went up the ladder first. The trap-door was heavy to push up. At last it opened and fell back.

Ben climbed into the attic. Max followed him. They looked round. The attic had one small window. There were a lot of cobwebs. The water-tank rumbled on one side. Boxes were stacked against the wall between the two houses. The light was dim.
It was a good place for a secret camp.

Ben had once been to the attic with his Dad.
Then his Dad had said he was not to go there alone.
Well, he wasn't alone with Max, was he?

Parts of the floor were boarded over.
The rest was just wooden beams with
plaster underneath. Dad had said it was easy
to make a hole in the plaster.

"We can make a camp on the boarded bit," Ben said. "I will fetch my cars. There isn't very much room but we can leave the toys up here."

They fetched the cars, the Lego and the comics.

"I know," said Ben. "I will write a note saying I am playing with you at your house, Max. Then if they come upstairs they won't know I am in the attic."

"Good idea," said Max.

Ben wrote the note and left it on the hall table.

Chapter 3: Waiting for Max

"We need food," said Max. "I'll go and fetch some biscuits, fizzy drinks, nuts and fruit from my house."

"Then we can stay in the attic for a long time," said Ben, who was always hungry. "Before you go, I will take the toys up into the roof," he said. "Then you bolt the trap-door and hook the ladder up. I shall be secret then."

Max bolted the trap-door and went to his house. "I won't be long," he called out.

Ben put the cars on the attic floor. He built a garage with the Lego.

Max was a long time. Ben felt hungry. He looked out of the small window. It was dirty and covered with cobwebs. It was raining outside in the street.

Ben thought he saw Max's Dad's van going down the street. It turned the corner and was gone. He sighed. Where was Max? It was boring here on his own.
He tried to read a comic by the window. Surely Max would come soon? He listened for footsteps. Nothing happened.

Ben wondered if Max had forgotten all about him.
Perhaps his mother would not let him come back.
Ben's parents would not know where he was.
They would think he was with Max.

Ben was very hungry now. He might starve
up here before they heard him call out.
He couldn't unbolt the trap-door from inside.

Chapter 4: Trapped!

Even if the trap-door was open, he would have to jump a long way down. Ben told himself he was too old to cry. After all, his parents must come upstairs when the shop was shut. Perhaps if he banged loudly someone might hear.

He banged on the trap-door. "Help!" he called. "I'm stuck up here! Mum! Dad!"

Nobody came. It was only just after dinner. It would be hours until the shop shut.

Why didn't Max come back? Ben went to the little window. Perhaps if he waved and called someone might see him. He waved but nobody looked up. How stupid he had been! It was silly letting himself be shut in.

Supposing there was a fire? Nobody would know he was there.

Perhaps he could find another way out. Ben walked round the attic. When he came to the end of the boarded part, he was careful only to step on the wooden beams. He did not want to fall through.

Just to stop himself crying, he moved some of the boxes. They were filled with old clothes, saucepans, and baby toys. Here was his old cot, behind the boxes. Here was his baby bath. He could not believe he had ever been small enough to lie in the cot or the bath.

He wondered if he should move all the boxes, but nobody had two trap-doors into the roof. Then he saw some different coloured paint. He moved another box.

There was a square of dirty paint covered in cobwebs. He looked closer. It was a door! Nobody had opened it for a long time.

The door had a rusty bolt. It must lead to Max's attic. Ben tried to move the bolt but it was stuck.

Chapter 5: Escape

Ben was so disappointed that he did cry, just a little. Mum always said: "If at first you don't succeed, try, try again." Well, he would try again.

He wriggled and pushed at the bolt. At last he felt it move, just a little. If only he had some oil.

He gave a big tug. The bolt shot back. He went through the little door into the next attic.

Max's attic was full of junk, just as Max had said. Ben saw boxes and cases and rolls of old carpet. The only light came through a little piece of glass in the roof. Nobody had put boards on this floor. It was all beams. He walked along them carefully until he came to a trap-door like the one in his attic.

Perhaps nobody would hear him. Perhaps Max's parents had shut the shop and they had all gone out.

"Help!" he called. "Max, where are you? It's your fault I'm shut in!"

Nobody came.

He took off his shoe and banged on the trap-door. He banged and banged until his arm ached. Again he nearly cried. Then suddenly he heard a voice.

"Who's that?" called Max's Dad.

"It's me! It's Ben!" Ben called.

He heard a clattering. Then the bolt was opened.

The trap-door was flung back. It knocked him off the beams. One of his feet went through the plaster.

"Oh!" cried Ben. He could not move! One leg had disappeared up to his knee!

"My ceiling!" said Max's Dad. He came up into the attic. He pulled Ben free and helped him down the ladder.

"Look what you have done," he said.

Ben saw the hole in the bathroom ceiling. Bits of plaster lay on the floor.

"I'm sorry," Ben said. "But I was shut in our attic. I found a door to yours. Where's Max?"

"His Gran was taken to hospital," said Max's father. "Max went with his Mum to see her. What were you doing in the attic?"

"Well, we had nowhere to play," Ben said. "That's why we went to our attic."

"I think you had better run home quickly," said Max's father. "Your mother has been here to look for you. I said you had not been in the house."

Ben was worried. She might have rung the Police.

Chapter 6: A great idea!

Ben met his mother on their doorstep. She was wearing a raincoat.

"I have been to the park to look for you," she said. They went through the shop.

"I'm sorry," Ben said. He told her what had happened.

"You told a lie in your note," Mum said. "It would have served you right if you had stayed up in the attic till tea."

Ben's father was angry when he heard that
Ben had put his foot through the ceiling next door.

"I will go and see Max's father when my shop
has shut," he said. "And you can come with me."

He gave Ben jobs to do in the shop until it shut,
instead of watching TV.

"That's your punishment!" he said.

Later they went to Max's house. Max and his mother
were just getting out of the van. Max stood still.
His mouth opened.

"Oh Ben!" he said. "I was so worried about my Gran.
I forgot about you!"

"I found a door from your attic to mine," Ben said.

"Gran's going to be all right," said Max's mother. "What do you mean, you forgot about Ben?"

They went inside and everyone explained all over again. Ben's father looked at the hole in the bathroom ceiling.

"It's a good thing you have a small foot," Dad said. "I shall come and put more plaster on the ceiling and then paint it," he said to Max's father.

"It was silly to go up into the attic," Mum said.

"There is no room in our house to play," Ben said. "And you don't like me to leave my train-set out."

"There's no room in our house either," said Max.

"Both attics would be lovely play-rooms," said Ben.

"Perhaps they do need more space to play," said Ben's father.

"Yes," agreed Max's parents.

"We are all so busy with our shops," said Ben's mother. "There's no time to tidy up toys all the day."

"It would mean clearing out all those boxes," said Max's mother.

"We could board over the floor in both attics," said Ben's father.

"Then nobody could fall through!" Max's mother laughed. Ben thought it was kind of her when she had a hole in her bathroom ceiling.

"And they will need electric light," said Max's father.

"We can help," Ben said.

"Yes, of course we can," said Max.

"It's a great idea!" said Ben.

The boys helped all they could.
They brushed away the cobwebs and the dirt.
They helped put the boards on the floors
over the beams. They helped take down
the old boxes and sort out the junk.
Ben's father made the little window open.

"It will be hot up here in the summer," he said.

The fathers fixed up the electric light points.
It took some time because they still had to
work in their shops.

At last it was done. Ben's Mum made some cakes. Max brought biscuits and fruit from the shop. Ben brought up comics from his parents' shop.

They took up the Lego, the toy cars and Max's model airplanes. They went up the ladder with jig-saws. Now they did not have to be put away before they were finished. They took up their water-pistols. Now nobody would mind about the splashes!

Last of all, they arranged the two electric train-sets on the floor. They could join up the lines now. Ben's joined Max's through the open door between the attics.

"We can send messages by train to each other," said Ben.

"No more mess!" said their mothers.

"I can play my music loudly up here," said Max. "It's great!"

"We shall be really private," said Ben. He fixed a notice to both ladders:
PRIVATE PROPERTY.
PLEASE KEEP OFF THE LINE!

When I'm grown up

I wonder what I would like to be.
A soldier, perhaps, in the queen's army.

I might be a nurse in an apron white,
To help heal the sick by day and night.

It might be fun to fly a plane,
To swoop to the sky and down again.

Maybe I'll swing on a high trapeze,
Flying above your heads with ease.

Perhaps I'll be a policeman tall,
I'll come and help whenever you call.

Perhaps I'll be a circus clown
Making you laugh when you're feeling down.

Sailors I know go off to sea,
Perhaps a sailor is what I'll be.

A fireman's job is a dangerous one,
For putting out fires is never fun.

There are so many things that I might be,
I'll wait a few years and then I'll see.

Peggy Clulow